Threads That Held Me Together

A Memoir by:
Natalie Woods
with Alexandria Roberts

a Silver Bangles Production

For permission requests, media inquiries, or bulk orders, please contact:
Silver Bangles Productions
info@silverbanglesproductions.com
www.silverbanglesproductions.com

Student Writer: Alexandria Roberts
Program Director & Publisher: Summer J. Robinson
Book Cover Design: Book Design Stars
Cover Photography: Davion Radford
Printed in Atlanta, Georgia, U.S.A.
First Edition, May 2026
Library of Congress Cataloging-in-Publication Data available on file
ISBN: 978-1-972235-03-4

Table of Contents

Foreword

Some friendships are seasonal. Others become woven into the fabric of your life. My friendship with Natalie Hall Williams Woods is the latter.

I have known Natalie since the third grade, and from the very beginning, she has been the kind of person who shows up fully for the people she loves. Loyal, dependable, and endlessly generous, Natalie has always been a true ride-or-die friend. Whether it was a simple road trip across town or a major life moment, she was there without hesitation.

Some of my earliest memories of Natalie take me back to the 1960s — riding in the backseat of my father's car on road trips, eating my mother's fried chicken and white Wonder Bread, laughing and talking the entire way. Natalie never cared whether something was exciting or glamorous; if it meant spending time together, she was all in.

Over the years, we shared so many beautiful moments growing up together. I remember us wearing pedal pusher shorts on fishing trips as little girls, matching long shirts and shiny red patent leather boots in elementary school, and later, getting dressed up to attend the Ebony Fashion Show as teenagers. Those memories still make me smile.

As adults, our friendship deepened even more. We grew from children eating bologna and grilled cheese sandwiches together into women sharing fine meals, many of them lovingly prepared by Natalie herself. To know Natalie is to know her gifts. She is an incredible cook, a talented seamstress, a hairstylist, and a deeply creative woman. When we were younger, she even made my junior prom dress by hand — a reflection of the care and love she pours into everything she does.

What I admire most about Natalie, though, is her consistency. Through births, weddings, graduations, illnesses, hospital stays, celebrations, and losses, she has always shown up. If you need Natalie, she is there. That kind of presence is rare.

Our circle of girlfriends has remained close since elementary and junior high school, and that in itself says something powerful about the kind of woman Natalie is. Decades later, we still gather together, laugh until we cry, and take our annual girls trips. Time has changed many things, but it has never changed Natalie's heart.

This memoir is a reflection of a life rooted in love, friendship, resilience, creativity, and community. I feel honored to have walked beside Natalie through so many chapters of her journey, and I am even more honored to introduce her story to you now.

As you read these pages, I hope you come to know the Natalie I have known and loved for so many years: a woman who gives deeply, loves generously, and leaves every space warmer than she found it.

-Desiree West | Realtor

Our family tree is rooted deep in the fertile soil of Mississippi.

Large, growing without limit, sheltering, and majestic.

The trunk of the tree is wide, gnarled, worn, and sturdy.

Each generation brings forth sprawling branches that sprout leaves of varying shades of green, signaling vitality and robust growth.

My mother was the first of her generation.

Natalie was the lastborn of the same generation.

Same family tree, different resplendent branches.

My mother named Natalie - it is a word of Latin origin, heralding the birth of Christ and the gift of salvation.

Natalie was born after the Feast of Thanksgiving, as the birth of Christ was to be celebrated. The name harkens and celebrates new beginnings.

Natalie is an integral part of our family tree.

Her vibrant branch of our tree is radiant and gorgeous in appearance and joie de vivre.

Natalie embodies spontaneity, a curiosity of spirit, dynamism, confidence, adventure, intelligence, passion, and warmth.

As she ages, she continues to shelter the younger branches of our family tree.

As they emerge, her canopy transforms in hue, shape, and color.

The trunk, branches, offshoots, leaves, and twigs of our shared weathered tree celebrate Natalie with heartfelt gratitude and love.

-Kimberly Toney Williams | Assistant District Attorney
and Natalie's cousin

Publisher's Note

Senior to Senior is an intergenerational storytelling program that pairs high school juniors and seniors with elders in the community to preserve oral histories, document lived experiences, and co-create professionally published memoirs.

At its core, this program is about memory, legacy, and connection. It is about slowing down long enough to truly listen to one another across generations. It is about honoring the stories that often go undocumented—the stories told in kitchens, on front porches, in church pews, beauty salons, workshops, family photo albums, and everyday conversation.

We are living in a time when history is constantly being revised, misrepresented, sanitized, and erased. Books are being banned. Cultural memory is disappearing. Elders are leaving this earth every day carrying entire libraries within them. At the same time, young people are searching for grounding, truth, identity, and deeper meaning in a world designed to keep us disconnected from ourselves, our histories, and one another.

Senior to Senior was created as a response to that disconnection.

I grew up around elders, both in my family and within my community. Some of my earliest and most meaningful memories are of sitting at the feet of my great-grandmother, Ruby Mae Jordan, listening to stories about her childhood, her family, her work, and the world she came from. Even into my college years, I found myself drawn to elders—their wisdom, humor, honesty, and perspective. I spent years deeply connected to my paternal grandparents and surrounded by older people who understood the value of memory and storytelling. Long before I understood the language for it, I understood that our elders carried something sacred.

But as I grew older, I also began to understand something equally important: wisdom does not only belong to elders.

Young people carry vision. Curiosity. Emotional honesty. Cultural awareness. Creativity. Courage. They ask difficult questions. They challenge systems and assumptions. They imagine futures that older generations may not yet be able to see. In many ways, young people are often deeply intuitive observers of the world around them.

Senior to Senior exists because I believe both generations need one another.

The elders offer memory, lived experience, survival, context, and reflection. The students offer fresh perspective, imagination, energy, technological fluency, and new ways of understanding the world. When they come together with openness and mutual respect, something transformative happens. The relationship stops being transactional and becomes reciprocal. The students are not simply "helping" elders tell their stories, and the elders are not simply "teaching" the students. They are learning each other.

Though I consciously created Senior to Senior out of my belief in storytelling and intergenerational healing, I now realize I was also being guided by someone who forever changed the course of my life: the late Dan Moore, Sr., founder of the APEX Museum, Atlanta's oldest and primary museum solely dedicated to preserving African American history and culture.

I met Mr. Moore in 2014, the summer before my senior year of high school. My grandmother, Lucy LaVoulle, took my brother and me to the APEX Museum before we left for a 25-day trip to Ghana and Ethiopia through HABESHA's *Back to Our Roots* program. Mr. Moore was thrilled to see two Black teenagers preparing to travel to Africa to learn, study, and reconnect with the diaspora.

He asked me what I was interested in, and I told him I loved reading, writing, and filmmaking. During that very first meeting, Mr. Moore walked back into his office, returned with a digital camera, placed it in my hands, and told me to document my journey in Africa. He then said something that would change my life: when I returned, he would help me write a book.

That fall, I returned to the APEX Museum as an intern, and true to his word, Mr. Moore taught me how to write and publish what became my first book, *Discovering Summer Abroad: A Teen's Journey to Africa.*

But perhaps even more importantly, he showed me that storytelling could be an act of preservation, healing, and service to others.

Less than six months later, Mr. Moore introduced me to a woman named Sheila Baltazar, whose son Patrick was one of the victims of the Atlanta Child Murders. She wanted her story—and her son's story—to be remembered. Mr. Moore looked at me, a seventeen-year-old high school senior, and told me that I should write her story.

At the time, I was shocked. Writing my own book had never been part of my plans, let alone writing someone else's life story. But Mr. Moore believed I could do it before I believed it myself.

He handed me a recorder and told me, simply, "Talk to her. Listen."

And that is what I did.

For weeks, I sat with Mrs. Baltazar listening to her memories—her childhood, her move to Atlanta, the unimaginable grief of losing her son, and the life she built despite that pain. We sat together in Mr. Moore's office at the museum talking for hours. I listened carefully, recorded everything, asked questions, and took notes. Then I went home and manually transcribed every interview word for word. At the time, I did not know transcription software existed. I simply understood that every word mattered.

Afterward, I shaped those conversations into narrative form. I did not yet know the term "memoir." I only knew that someone trusted me enough to tell me their story, and that I had a responsibility to honor it with care.

I was still only seventeen years old.

That experience taught me something I have carried ever since: young people are far more capable than society often gives them credit for, and elders are far more eager to share their stories than we often realize. What is missing is intentional space for those two groups to come together in meaningful, human ways.

Senior to Senior is that space.

This program exists because of the elders who raised me, the community that poured into me, and mentors like Mr. Moore who showed me what becomes possible when we trust young people with meaningful work and create environments where generations can truly see one another.

Every book created through this program is more than a

memoir. It is an archive. A bridge between generations. A refusal to allow stories to disappear. A declaration that ordinary lives are worthy of documentation and remembrance.

These pages are proof that storytelling is not just art, it is preservation. It is resistance. It is healing. And perhaps most importantly, it is how we remember one another, and ourselves.

In community and remembrance,
Summer J. Robinson
Creator of Senior to Senior:
An Interngenerational Storytelling Program
Founder & Publisher, Silver Bangles Productions

About the Project

This book was created through *Senior to Senior:* An Intergenerational Storytelling Program founded by Summer J. Robinson through Silver Bangles Productions.

From September 2025 through January 2026, high school juniors and seniors met twice a week with elders in the community to listen, learn, and document their life stories. Using a guided interview process, students asked questions about childhood, family, love, work, faith, loss, joy, survival, memory, and legacy. The elders shared openly, while students listened carefully, recorded conversations, and followed the natural flow of storytelling with additional questions and reflection.

What began as conversation slowly became archive.

From February through May 2026, students transcribed hours of recorded interviews and worked to identify the deeper narrative themes woven throughout their partner's life. From there, they developed chapter outlines and shaped the interviews into memoir form.

Throughout the writing process, the elders remained active collaborators. At multiple stages, they returned to review drafts, clarify timelines, expand details, correct information, and ensure their voice and experiences were being represented honestly and authentically. The books were not written *about* the elders, but *with* them.

This collaborative process is what makes each Senior to

Senior book unique.

These memoirs are not celebrity stories or distant historical accounts. They are living histories rooted in everyday people whose lives carry extraordinary wisdom, memory, and meaning. They preserve personal and community history that may otherwise go undocumented.

At a time when generations are increasingly disconnected, Senior to Senior creates space for relationship, mutual learning, and understanding. The students brought curiosity, creativity, patience, and fresh perspective. The elders brought lived experience, reflection, humor, resilience, and historical memory. Together, they created something neither generation could have created alone.

Each book in this series stands as both a memoir and an archive—a testament to the power of storytelling, listening, and intergenerational connection.

Dedication

To my family—past and present—thank you for being
the foundation of my story.

To my mother, who worked hard and held our home together, thank you for your strength.

To my friends, some of whom have been with me since
childhood, thank you for your loyalty and love.

To my husband, thank you for walking beside me through
life and building a lasting partnership.

And to every experience that shaped me, even the difficult
ones,
I acknowledge your place in my growth.

This is my story, and I offer it with love to those
who come after me.

With all my love,
Natalie Woods

Sunnydale Rhythms:
The Geometry of the Blocks

The world of my early childhood was measured in concrete and community, bounded by the stark, repetitive architecture of the Sunnydale projects in San Francisco. To an outsider, Sunnydale might have looked like a place defined by its edges—a series of uniform, boxy blocks tucked into the city's southeastern pocket, shadowed by the looming hills. But to a child of six, it was a sprawling, vibrant kingdom.

It had its own atmosphere, a specific "rhythm" composed of the rhythmic slap-slap of double-dutch ropes, the distant, metallic hum of the Muni transit buses, and the steady, guiding pulse of a family trying to carve out a life of dignity in a space designed for utility. The buildings were painted in muted, institutional tones, but the life between them was a riot of color.

The Law of the Living Room

In my mother's house, that rhythm was dictated by a very specific frequency: silence. We were raised under the firm, traditional mandate that children were to be "seen and not heard." This wasn't a suggestion; it was the law of the land.

In the projects, where the walls were thin enough to hear a neighbor's cough and the world outside was a constant roar of car engines and shouting, my mother maintained our household through a quiet, steel-spined discipline. She didn't need to raise her voice. A single look—a sharpening of the eyes or a subtle tilt of the chin—was enough to bring the room to a standstill.

We learned to be observers. While my older sister, the "borderline genius," occupied space with her intellect and her volume, I became a student of the unspoken. I watched the way the afternoon light hit the linoleum kitchen table, revealing the scratches of a thousand meals. I

studied the way my mother moved with a purposeful grace even when her shoulders were heavy with the exhaustion of a double shift. I learned to read the shift in a voice or the set of a shoulder long before I was ever invited into the conversation. It was a training ground for empathy, teaching me to navigate a world that wasn't always kind by understanding it before I entered it.

The Symphony of the "Four Corners"

Stepping out of the curated quiet of our apartment and into the common areas of Sunnydale was like moving from a black-and-white film into Technicolor. The air changed. It became thick with the scents of a dozen different lives: the sharp tang of frying fish, the heavy sweetness of laundry detergent from the communal mats, and the metallic tang of the fog rolling in from the Bay.

The heart of our social world was the "four corners." These weren't just intersections of asphalt and cracked sidewalk; they were the stages where the drama of the neighborhood played out. You had:

The Elders: The women who traded news over brown paper grocery bags, their voices a low murmur of warnings and "did you hear?"

The Sentinels: The older boys who stood on the corners, leaning against lamp posts with a practiced, leaning coolness. They were the keepers of the gate, their eyes scanning the street for anything that didn't belong.

The Playground Kings: For us, the corners were the invisible boundaries of our kingdom. We played street games with a fierce, joyful intensity. Whether it was tag, jump rope, or games of our own invention that turned a cracked sidewalk into a palace. We claimed the asphalt as our own.

The Secret Language of the Telephone

Despite the "survival" aspect of living in the projects, there was an undeniable lightness to our childhood. We found ways to be mischievous that felt like high-stakes spy missions. Because we were meant to be unheard in the house, our voices became our most potent tools of rebellion.

I still vividly remember the collective breath we'd hold around the rotary telephone. Our fingers would tremble with adrenaline as we dialed a random number, the plastic wheel clicking back into place with agonizing slowness.

"Is your refrigerator running?" we'd whisper, our hearts hammering against our ribs.

"Yes..." the confused, unsuspecting voice would reply.

"Well, you better go catch it!"

We would slam the phone down and erupt into a fit of silent, shoulder-shaking giggles. We had to be silent—if my mother heard, the "seen and not heard" rule would be enforced with a quickness—but the internal roar of our laughter was deafening. In those moments, we weren't just kids in the projects; we were pranksters, creators of chaos, throwing our voices into the San Francisco night just to prove we existed.

The Great Migration: Leaving the Box
The rhythm of Sunnydale eventually shifted into the heavy thud of cardboard boxes and the screech of a moving truck. When I was about seven, the era of the projects came to an end. We weren't just moving; we were ascending. We were headed to our first real home—a house with a backyard and a deed.
The transition felt seismic. I remember the sheer, electric excitement of walking into that new space. Even though I still shared a room with my sister, the air felt different. It didn't smell like the neighbor's cooking or the communal hallway. It smelled like us.
There was a backyard where the grass was ours to cut, a sense of privacy that felt like a luxury, and a quiet that didn't feel enforced by thin walls, but earned by my mother's tireless work. It was our first taste of "the dream," a tangible step toward a life that felt limitless.

The Foundation of the Fog

Looking back, Sunnydale wasn't just a place I lived; it was the place that built me. It gave me my first set of tools for the world. It taught me how to navigate diversity without fear, how to find joy in the smallest pockets of life, and how to maintain a sense of self in a crowded room.

Those "Sunnydale rhythms"—the balance of discipline and play, of silence and laughter—remained etched into my foundation. They were the first lessons in resilience, preparing me for the many cities I would eventually see from 30,000 feet up, and the many lives I was yet to lead. I was Natalie, a girl from the projects who had learned to listen to the world before she decided to speak to it.

The Kitchen Duel

The air in my mother's kitchen was thick—not with the usual sweet, heavy aroma of her phenomenal sweet potato pies, but with a tension so sharp you could nearly see it shimmering above the stove like a heat haze. Although we were no longer in Sunnydale and in our new home, we had a lot more room to breathe, that afternoon, the kitchen felt smaller than a closet.

My sister, eleven years my senior, occupied that space like a storm front. She moved through the world with a "borderline genius" IQ and a voice that demanded every ear in the room. Growing up, I was her shadow, the "meek and mild" youngest child. While she played the brilliant, boisterous center of attention, I played the quiet observer. We were raised on the mantra that children were to be "seen and not heard," and I had played that part to perfection for years, fading into the wallpaper whenever her drama reached a crescendo.

Until that afternoon.

She was hovering over a heavy iron skillet, the oil popping and hissing as she prepared a meal for her boyfriend, Carl. I was a teenager then, perpetually hungry and weary of navigating the unspoken territorial boundaries of our crowded home. To me, the food on the counter wasn't a romantic gesture; it was just a snack in my own house. I didn't think twice; I reached for a piece of fried chicken.

The reaction was instantaneous. My sister, with her signature long, manicured nails, didn't just snap at me—she slapped the chicken right out of my hand, her movements jagged and violent.

"I cooked this for Carl," she hissed. Her eyes, usually bright with intellect, were now flashing with a raw, territorial fire. "Not for you."

She didn't just stop me; she snatched the food out of my hand and tossed it back into the skillet with a splash of hot grease.

In that moment, something shifted in the very molecules of that small San Francisco kitchen. The "meek and mild" girl vanished. The decades of being the shadow, the silent observer of her genius and her whims, evaporated in the heat of the stove. I didn't see a brilliant older sister anymore; I saw a boundary that had been crossed one too many times.

I didn't argue. I didn't cry. I didn't retreat into the hallway as I had a thousand times before. I swung. I punched her right there in the middle of the kitchen, the impact vibrating up my arm.

We went at it—two sisters duking it out on the laminate flooring in my mother's galley-shaped kitchen, a blur of motion, flying hair, and those long, sharp nails. I remember the stinging heat on my face where she scratched me, and she too had a battle scar that never disappeared, the metallic taste of adrenaline, but I didn't back down. I couldn't. Every year of being ignored or pushed aside fueled my grip.

The noise must have been deafening, because Carl had to rush downstairs to break us up. He pulled us apart, his hands like anchors on our shoulders as we both breathed heavily, our chests heaving in rhythm. The silence that followed was even louder than the scuffle—a heavy, ringing quiet that signaled the end of an era.

It was the first and only physical fight we ever had, but

it was the most important moment of my young life. Looking at her then, disheveled and shocked, I realized that being "smart" wasn't enough if you used that intelligence to diminish the people around you. She was a genius who wanted to be taken care of; I was a girl who had just realized I could take care of myself.

That scratch on my face eventually healed into a faint, thin line that only I could see in the mirror, but the internal change was permanent. I had set a boundary in the most literal, visceral way possible. I wasn't just the "little sister" anymore. I was Natalie.

And as I looked out the window, I knew that if I could stand my ground in that kitchen, I could eventually stand my ground anywhere in the world. The world was large, loud, and often unkind, but I finally had my own voice to answer it.

The Shadow of the Womanizer
The Architect of Silence

My mother moved through the kitchen with a rhythmic, percussive energy—the sharp snap of a dish towel, the heavy thud of a cast-iron skillet, the piercing whistle of a coffee pot. These were the sounds that filled the space where conversation should have been. Her silence was its own kind of loud, a constant frequency that hummed with the stress of keeping our world from collapsing. She was a woman of fierce, bordering on territorial, protection. Every bolt on the door and every stern look was a brick in the fortress she built around us. To her, information was a liability; the less we knew about the chaos outside—or the complications of our own bloodline—the safer we were. But safety felt a lot like isolation.

The Legend of the "Womanizer"

Then there was my father—the "Womanizer." It's a heavy, jagged word for a child to carry, a title that implies a surplus of love given everywhere except where it was needed most. I felt the true meaning of that name in the vast, hollow gaps he left behind: the empty chairs at birthdays, the quiet phone that never rang on Sunday mornings, the missed graduations.

To see him was a rare, choreographed event, less like a family visit and more like a high-stakes diplomatic summit.

These visits were held in our small living room, an arena where the air grew thick with unspoken history. My mother would sit in the corner, her posture as rigid as a sentinel, her eyes never leaving him. The television would be off, making every creak of the floorboards sound like a gunshot.

I remember the way he'd walk into that room, the very air seemingly shifting its molecular structure to accommodate him. His presence vibrated with a magnetic, dangerous charm—a polished, effortless charisma that could make you feel like the only person in the universe for a fleeting second. He'd lean in, smelling of expensive cologne and the world outside, his eyes locked on yours with an intensity that felt like a promise. He'd laugh, and for a moment, it felt like any worries were thousands of miles away. But that light was a spotlight, not a hearth; it didn't provide warmth, only visibility. As soon as he stepped back out into the San Francisco mist, the darkness felt twice as heavy and the night air twice as biting as before. He was a master of the exit, leaving us to navigate the shadows he cast.

The Fractured Branches

The real mystery, however, lay in the seven brothers I barely knew—seven branches of the same tree, growing in completely different directions, shaded by thickets of secrets and half-truths. We shared a name and a lineage, yet we were strangers bound by a bloodline that felt more like a labyrinth than a bridge.

I'd catch glimpses of them sometimes—a familiar tilt of a head in a crowd, a shared jawline in a fading photograph— but we were separated by more than just distance. We were separated by the "invisible walls" my mother built. To her, every brother was a potential link back to a life she was trying to outrun. We navigated the same city, perhaps even crossed the same streets, but we were ghost ships passing in the fog of the Bay.

The Night of the Storm

The deepest shadow of all was the "lost" baby brother. For years, he was a ghost in our genealogy, a name whispered only when the wind was high and the house was still. As the story goes - my baby brother's mother, my fathers now second wife, had to flee in the middle of the night to give birth to my baby brother, the relentless thrum of the rain against the roof on the night she vanished. The sound was a frantic, irregular heartbeat, mirroring the panic unfolding all she went through with my father within the walls of where they lived. Gloria had to run from the abuse of my father. It wasn't until my forties that one of my father's sons, Ricky, who was now blind due to diabetes, set out to find our baby brother. Ricky was able to find him by the grace of god. By this time in Ricky's life he had become a minister. He let all his siblings know that he was able to find little Louis. Even though my father was abusive, Gloria named her son after his father.

I remember the front door swinging open, inviting the damp chill of the night inside. My mother fled into that storm, her silhouette a sharp, desperate outline against the grey San Francisco mist. The streetlights caught the raindrops like falling glass as she disappeared into the gloom. When she returned hours later, she was different—colder, more resolute, her eyes turned to flint. A piece of our collective history had gone with her into the night, buried under the weight of a fifty-year silence. You see, my parents never married. My father was a man who had to have a woman in his life, and not always for the right reason. I believe that my mother either experienced the rath of my father or came to a conclusion that she was not going to tolerate any kind of abuse from the likes of Louis Hall. Later in life I asked mom what happened between the two of them, but I never got an answer.

The Breaking of the 50-Year Silence

That silence didn't just end; it shattered. For decades, I looked at the moon and wondered if he was staring at that same glowing from some distant porch, wondering about the sisters he never knew. I imagined a thousand different lives for him: Was he happy? Was he angry? Did he even know we existed?

The truth finally began to trickle out in fragments—a stray comment from an elder, a document found in the bottom of a cedar chest, a phone call that changed the gravity of my world. It was a slow, painful exhumation of a life that had been intentionally erased. Finding him wasn't like the movies; there were no swelling violins, just the stark, quiet realization that a man had been living a whole life while we had been mourning a ghost.

From the Projects to the Desert

It wasn't until many years later, standing under the vast, indifferent sky of a desert horizon in Saudi Arabia, that my perspective finally shifted. In the absolute silence of the dunes, thousands of miles away from the rain-slicked streets of San Francisco, the heat of the desert seemed to bake away the fog of my childhood. I realized that some things don't just get lost in the shuffle of life. Sometimes, things are hidden with intentional, agonizing precision. They are buried deep in the soil of the past—not out of malice or forgetfulness, but as a final, desperate act of love to keep the rest of us safe from the storm that took them.

Halloween and Higher Altitudes

The fog of San Francisco had always been a physical manifestation of the boundaries of my world. It kept the worries tucked away, a self-contained universe of iron-clad rules and silent survival. But by the time I reached the threshold of my twenties, the air in the city felt thin, not from altitude, but from a lack of space to grow. Although I had had that experience with my sister, I was still seen as that "meek and mild" girl, the one who moved through the world with a quiet caution, reflecting the "seen and not heard" upbringing that had been my armor for so long.

Then came Halloween night. While the rest of the world was donning masks to become someone else, I was preparing for an interview that would finally allow me to take mine off. My sister-in-law had been the one to plant the seed, suggesting I apply to World Airways. It wasn't just any airline; it was a major charter carrier that held the largest military contract in the country. The stakes felt monumental. I walked into that interview as a girl from the projects and walked out as a trainee for an international career.

The Flight of the 21st Year

Training was a seven-week whirlwind of emergency protocols, cabin management, and the rigorous standards of international service. It was a metamorphosis. The meek girl who avoided conflict had to learn how to command a cabin, manage a diverse crew, and eventually, handle the complexities of international passengers.

A significant milestone occurred right as those five weeks drew to a close: I turned twenty-one. In the world of aviation, this wasn't just a birthday; it was a professional certification. Reaching that age meant I was finally legally allowed to serve alcohol on board. It felt like the final seal on my adulthood. I was no longer just a girl traveling; I was a professional responsible for the comfort and safety of hundreds of people as we crossed oceans.

Managing the Global Cabin

World Airways took me far beyond the reach of the San Francisco mist. We weren't just flying tourists to vacation spots; we were flying military troops and their dependents to every corner of the globe. This exposure was my true education. While the neighborhood I grew up in was being devastated by the drug culture of the era, I was navigating the streets of foreign capitals. The job became my sanctuary and my bridge to the rest of the world. It allowed me to bypass the traps that had claimed so many of my peers, replacing the limited horizon of the projects with the infinite view from thirty thousand feet.

I transitioned from someone who followed the rules to someone who enforced them with grace. Managing an international cabin required a level of emotional intelligence I hadn't realized I possessed. I had to learn the nuances of different cultures, the quiet art of de-escalating tension in a cramped metal tube, and the stamina to remain "on" for fourteen-hour hauls across the Atlantic and Pacific.

The Shadow of the Desert

Working for a military contractor during global conflicts meant the job wasn't always glamour and layovers. The reality of the "Project Landscape" I had escaped was replaced by the high-stakes landscape of international geopolitics. I remember one harrowing flight during Desert Storm when our routine took a terrifying turn. We were scheduled to land at a specific base, but through a series of errors, we touched down at the wrong airport in an Arab country.

The moment the doors opened, the "magnetic charm" of my father's world or the quiet safety of my mother's kitchen felt a million miles away. We weren't met by ground crew or shuttle buses; we were met by military personnel with rifles leveled at the aircraft. Standing in the doorway of that plane, looking out at the desert heat and the barrels of those guns, I realized how far I had come. I was no longer the girl who was "seen and not heard." I was the one who had to stay calm, lead the crew, and navigate a situation where a single mistake could have international consequences.

A New Horizon

Ultimately, World Airways gave me more than just a career and a way out; it gave me the foundation of my future. It was in that high-altitude world that I met a pilot who would eventually become my husband. The "Shadow of the Womanizer" that had defined my understanding of men was replaced by a partnership built on shared skies and mutual respect.

Looking back, that Halloween night wasn't just a big break. It was the moment the silence of my childhood was replaced by the roar of jet engines. I had climbed above the fog, finding a clarity that only comes when you're brave enough to leave the ground behind.

The Cockpit & Kiss

The transition from the "meek and mild" girl of Sunnydale to a seasoned international flight attendant was not just about mastering safety protocols or serving fine spirits at thirty thousand feet, it was about discovering a world where I could finally breathe, and more importantly, it was about finding the partner who would navigate those ever-changing skies with me. The trajectory of my life shifted during a long-haul flight for World Airways, a change that began with something as simple and human as a pair of aching feet.

A Sanctuary Above the Clouds

On a particularly grueling trip—the kind where the hours stretch into an unrecognizable blur of time zones and the recycled air begins to feel like a weight—my feet were absolutely killing me. The constant movement through the narrow, vibrating aisles of the cabin had taken its toll, and I desperately needed a moment of reprieve. I found myself seeking refuge in the one place on the aircraft that felt like a quiet sanctuary: the cockpit.

At the time, the cockpit was a place of focused, technical calm, bathed in the soft glow of instrument panels. As I stepped inside, the hum of the engines provided a rhythmic backdrop to the quiet efficiency of the crew. I must have looked as exhausted as I felt because the man in the pilot's seat looked back at me with a genuine, disarming kindness. We began to talk—not about flight paths, wind shear, or the logistics of the military charter, but about life. He noticed my discomfort and, in a gesture that completely bypassed the usual professional distance, offered to rub my feet.

It was a moment of vulnerability and unexpected tenderness that cut through the sterile exhaustion of the job. In that cramped space high above the Atlantic, the "Shadow of the Womanizer" that had loomed over my childhood began to dissipate. Here was a man who saw me—not as a "seen and not heard" child or a nameless crew member—but as a person who needed a moment of care. He offered a different kind of strength than I had known: one that didn't demand attention but provided a steady, quiet support.

The Sicily Bus Stop

Our romance, born in the pressurized quiet of the cockpit, quickly found its footing on the ground in ways that felt like scenes from a classic film. One of the most enduring memories of our early days together became known as the "Sicily Bus Stop." We were on separate crew assignments, our paths crossing only briefly on the sun-drenched island of Sicily. The air smelled of salt and citrus, a sharp contrast to the jet fuel and galley coffee that usually defined our meetings.

As our respective crew buses were preparing to depart in opposite directions for the airport, the realization that we were about to be separated by thousands of miles and weeks of scheduling hit us both. Without a second thought, we managed to get both buses to come to a screeching halt in the middle of a narrow Sicilian road. I stepped off my bus and as he looked out the window of his bus, he noticed I had made my way across a four lane busy road. We met in the dusty heat for a single, cinematic kiss. The rest of the crew watched from the windows—some cheering, some rolling their eyes—a captive audience to a moment of pure, unscripted devotion. It was a declaration that no matter where the job took us, we would find a way to bridge the distance.

35

The Long Runway Home:
Baltimore to California

BWI became the backdrop for eight formative years of our relationship. In Baltimore, we weren't just two people flying in opposite directions; we were building a home. We learned the rhythms of a city with a different kind of grit than San Francisco—a place of brick row houses and cold winters. It was there that we navigated the challenges of balancing two demanding aviation schedules, often passing each other like ships in the night at BWI airport.

The trajectory of our lives eventually swung westward again, landing us in Southern California. For eleven years, we lived under the bright sun and the fast-paced energy of the West Coast. It was a far cry from the rain-slicked streets of my youth in Sunnydale. I traded the fog of the Bay for the sprawling freeways of the Southland. Each move was a new chapter, a new set of streets to learn, and a new community to build. Yet, despite the beauty of the coast and the professional successes we found there, there was a persistent pull toward something more grounded, something that felt less like a layover and more like a final destination.

The Forever Landing

We eventually found our "forever" landing spot back in Georgia. Moving to the South wasn't just another relocation; it was a deliberate choice to find a home that offered a sense of permanence. In Georgia, the frantic energy of my early career and the constant movement of our younger years finally settled into a lasting peace.

Standing on our own land, surrounded by the lush green of the Georgia landscape, I realized that the journey from the projects to the cockpit had always been leading me here. I had spent years managing international cabins and navigating the complex "project landscape" of my past, but in this "forever" spot, I finally found a place where I didn't have to keep moving. I was no longer a ghost ship in the fog or a traveler between time zones; I was a woman firmly anchored in a life built on a foundation of love, shared skies, and the quiet joy of finally being home.

Mystery Missions and Machine Guns

In the early 1990s, the world felt like it was shifting on its axis, and I found myself vibrating at the very center of that spin. For years, the sky had been a sanctuary of predictable luxury—the scent of expensive perfumes in First Class, the gentle chime of call buttons, and the cosmopolitan hum of passengers discussing their upcoming stays in London, Paris, or Rome. But as the conflict in the Middle East escalated, the cabin was stripped of its softness. The plushness was replaced by a heavy, bureaucratic silence that felt like a physical weight against the eardrums, a pressure that no amount of altitude adjustment could pop.

There were no flight manifests shared in advance anymore. The era of knowing your destination before you zipped your suitcase was over. There was no casual banter in the galley about which Parisian bistro had the best steak and frites or which hotel in Frankfurt had the softest linens. Instead, there was the "Envelope." It was a standard-issue manila packet, unremarkable to a postal clerk, but to the crew of World Airways, it held the weight of an oracle. I recall the mid-air ritual with a sharp, lingering clarity that the passing decades haven't dimmed. Somewhere high over the dark, churning expanse of the Atlantic, as the rhythmic hum of the engines masked the uneasy, shallow breathing of the crew, the Captain would call the senior flight attendants to the flight deck.

The ritual was always the same: the snap of the thick,

red wax seal breaking, the rustle of heavy bond paper, and a sudden, sharp intake of breath that seemed to suck the oxygen out of the cockpit. Inside were the coordinates and the mission directives that would dictate their lives for the next forty-eight hours. The psychological weight of that moment—the literal "unfolding" of their fate at thirty-thousand feet—became a core part of my burgeoning resilience. You couldn't argue with the paper; you couldn't negotiate with the mission. You could only prepare your spirit for wherever it was sending you.

When the coordinates finally whispered "Saudi Arabia," the air in the cabin seemed to thin. The landing at the King's Airport was a sensory assault that redefined my understanding of "space." Back home, the "open" feeling of America meant a sky that felt limitless and safe, a horizon that promised opportunity and the freedom of the road. In the desert, that openness was terrifying. It was a landscape of blinding, white-hot sand and cold, industrial steel. There was no "welcome" here; there was only "clearance."

As the aircraft taxied toward a remote, isolated corner of the airfield, far from the civilian terminals, I leaned toward the small, scratched porthole. I didn't see baggage carts, fuel trucks, or the familiar neon-vested ground crew waving orange wands. Instead, I saw rows of soldiers standing in the shimmering heat haze, their faces obscured by tactical gear and the fine, tan dust of the desert. Most jarring were the matte-black barrels of the rifles—hundreds of them—pointed directly at the belly and the windows of the aircraft as it rolled to a heavy, shuddering stop.

The contrast was a lightning strike to my system. The "meek and mild" girl who had navigated the housing projects of Sunnydale, who had learned to be "seen and not heard" in my mother's house, was now a woman navigating a literal war zone. In this environment, I was more than just a crew member; I was a cultural friction point. I was a female leader in a space where my very presence, my uncovered hair, and my authoritative voice were challenges to the local order. I realized in those moments, standing at the door of the aircraft as the 110-degree heat of the desert rushed in to meet me, that I could no longer rely on the protections of my old life. I learned to move with a quiet, steely authority—a posture that commanded respect without needing to ask for it. In a world defined by machine guns, sealed envelopes, and mystery missions, I discovered that my voice—steady, clear, and unshakeable—was the only true weapon I had left to carry.

The TSA Frontier

If the Desert Storm years were a high-altitude test of survival in a world of external shadows, the aftermath of September 11, 2001, was a grounded test of creation in a world that had suddenly, violently, lost its sense of safety. For me, the transition from the clouds to the terminal floor was more than a change in altitude; it was a shift in identity. I was there at the absolute genesis of the Transportation Security Administration (TSA), stepping into a void where a national security apparatus needed to be built from scratch. It was a time of frantic, high-stakes improvisation—a period where the word "security" was being redefined in real-time, on the fly, and under the watchful, terrified eyes of the American public.

There were no legacy handbooks to consult in those early days. There were no dusty binders on shelves labeled "The Way We've Always Done It" to fall back on when things got complicated. Instead, there was only a desperate, collective national heartbeat of fear and an urgent, non-negotiable demand for a return to safety. I helped build the agency from the ground up, starting in the trenches of the checkpoints where the air was thick with tension and moving steadily into the complex, often grinding machinery of federal supervision. I wasn't just an employee; I was an architect of a new normal.

The "Daily Grind" of the 4:00 AM shift became both my sanctuary and my forge. There is a specific, eerie intimacy to an airport three hours before the sun comes up. I described the pre-dawn atmosphere with a visceral clarity: the sharp, metallic tang of ozone emanating from the hulking X-ray machines, the lukewarm, acidic taste of industrial coffee in a stained foam cup, and the rhythmic, hollow sound of footsteps echoing through a terminal that would soon be a sea of chaos. I watched the first wave of travelers—anxious, weary, and confused—as they learned to navigate a strange new world of removed shoes, discarded liquids, and the invasive hum of metal detectors.

But as my career progressed into leadership, my focus shifted. I realized that while the machinery was important, the mission lived or died with the human beings wearing the blue uniforms. I took my role as a supervisor personally—almost maternally. To me, I wasn't just auditing search techniques or checking badges; I was checking in on the souls of my team. I understood that a distracted officer was a dangerous one, and I knew that distraction usually started at home.

In the quiet, stolen moments between the heavy morning "pushes"—those brief windows when the terminal became a temporary vacuum of silence—I would gather the officers. They were a mosaic of the American workforce: young kids in their first government roles, eyes wide with the gravity of the badge, and older workers who had been displaced by a changing economy, looking for a final landing spot. I didn't just talk to them about prohibited items or the fine points of a pat-down; I talked to them about their lives, their dreams, and their fears.

I became a self-appointed financial chaplain in the breakroom. Amidst the crumbs of vending machine snacks and the hum of the refrigerator, I preached the gospel of the TSP (Thrift Savings Plan). I would sit with an officer and explain the magic of compound interest and the necessity of financial literacy, often with more passion than I used to explain security protocols. I understood a fundamental truth about leadership: to me, for officers to be truly vigilant at the checkpoint, they needed to feel secure in their own futures. If they were worrying about rent, they weren't looking for the threat.

I was teaching them that leadership wasn't about the power inherent in a brass badge or the authority to bark orders. It was about the heavy, quiet responsibility of the person wearing it. This chapter of my life chronicleed my own internal metamorphosis: my transition from a passenger in the world's grand, sweeping events to the one holding the line on the ground. I found a deep, rhythmic purpose in the discipline of service—a quiet, unsung labor that kept a nation moving when it was too afraid to stand still. I wasn't just securing flights; I was securing the confidence of a country, one person and one TSP contribution at a time.

Six Times a Realtor

Retirement from the federal government was marketed to me as a finish line—a well-earned exhale after decades of high-alert living, constant vigilance, and the heavy, invisible mantle of leadership. It was supposed to be the "Art of the Slow Down," a time for quiet mornings and a predictable, rhythmic pace. But for a woman whose spirit was forged in the "four corners" of Sunnydale and tempered in the high-stakes war zones of the Middle East, a finish line was merely a place to catch my breath before beginning a new, perhaps more frustrating, marathon. The transition into the Georgia real estate market wasn't just a career change; it was a humbling, grueling gauntlet that tested the very foundations of the resilience I had spent over fifty years building.

The heart of this chapter—and perhaps the defining metaphor for my later years—is the "Six Times" struggle. On paper, the real estate exam used to high stakes, complex federal regulations, and the crushing pressure of a ticking clock. Yet, the Georgia state real estate exam became a Goliath that seemed determined to break my spirit in a way that no military mission ever could.

Failing the exam the first time was an annoyance, a minor dent in my professional pride. Failing it a second and third time felt like a personal affront. By the fourth and fifth attempts, the failure began to feel like a heavy, suffocating blanket. I recount the lonely, late nights at my kitchen table in

Georgia, the yellow glow of a single lamp illuminating stacks of practice tests and neon-highlighted law books that felt like they were written in a foreign tongue. The frustration was visceral—the "fickle" nature of the multiple-choice questions that felt designed to trip up the experienced, and the "dumb" mistakes that kept my just points away from a passing grade. It was an ego-bruising reality check that I had lost my edge.

Passing on the sixth attempt wasn't just about obtaining a plastic license to sell houses; it was a hard-fought testament to my lifelong refusal to be defeated by a temporary setback. It was Sunnydale grit showing up in a quiet, sterile testing center. It was the "meek and mild" girl proving that my capacity was not defined by a score, but by the fact that I was willing to show up a sixth time when most would have walked away after the third.

Once I finally stepped out into the field, however, the battle shifted from the classroom to the red clay of South Fulton. I described the physical transformation of my community with a sharp, observant eye that only a resident can possess. The Amazon warehouses began to rise like windowless, concrete monoliths over the horizon of the West End, their sheer, gray scale threatening to swallow the historical character of the neighborhoods I remembered during my first taste of Atlanta. To me, these weren't just signs of economic progress; they were encroaching giants that risked erasing the stories of the people who lived there—the very people I had pledged to serve.

In the streets of Georgia, I saw the "fickle" nature of humanity firsthand. I dealt with buyers who would back out of a life-changing deal over a minor aesthetic detail like a chipped bathroom tile or a paint color they didn't like, seemingly oblivious to the structural integrity of the home. I met sellers who were so disconnected from the value of their own history that they were willing to trade a generational legacy for a quick check. My work wasn't just about "closings" or "new arrivals" who only saw an investment opportunity. I fought for the integrity of Atlanta, helping families find their "forever" landing spots in Georgia, just as I had finally found mine after a lifetime of travel and transition.

I later realized a profound truth: whether I was in a cockpit over the Atlantic, standing guard at a high-pressure security checkpoint in Atlanta, or sitting in a quiet, sun-drenched living room in the West End, my mission had never actually changed. I was, and had always been, the steady hand, the calm presence, and the unshakeable voice in a world that never stops changing.

A Life Unfolding:
The $400 Lettuce and the Mountain Cabin

We often labor under the dangerous, youthful delusion that the most profound lessons arrive with dramatic fanfare—that wisdom is gifted to us in moments of monumental climax. But the truth, I've found, is usually whispered in the quiet, mundane, and occasionally humiliating mishaps of travel. We look for enlightenment in grand cathedrals or on the peaks of mountains, only to find that our greatest teachers are the mistakes we make while trying to feed ourselves or find our way home.

Take, for instance, the time I found myself looking for a restaurant/ hotel in Sydney Australia to view the fireworks display for New Years Eve, staring down at a restaurant bill that hovered somewhere around $400 per person. To this day, it feels like that entire bill was for nothing more than a head of lettuce and a bit of hope. It was a laughable, stinging realization of being catastrophically unprepared. In that moment of sticker shock, a simple, iron-clad mantra was forged: *Book before you go.*

It is more than just a logistical rule for a traveler; it is a philosophy of existence. It represents the necessity of foresight in a world that thrives on chaotic unpredictability. If you do not plan for the mountain, the mountain will tax you in ways you didn't anticipate. Whether it is a kitchen budget or a life plan, the principle remains the same: you cannot arrive at your destination if you refuse to acknowledge the cost of the journey.

That lesson, however, was only the beginning of my education in my travels. In those learning moments, the frantic, buzzing pace of the modern world finally dissolved. I found myself sharing space with an independent soul of a dog named Buster. He possessed a rare, enviable quality—the ability to simply be. He understood something we humans spend our entire lives struggling to master: the art of waiting.

He would sit on that porch, entirely content in his own presence, watching the mist roll over the ancient trees as if he were the only creature in existence. Watching him, I realized that I had spent years in a perpetual state of "becoming," always rushing toward the next flight or the next career milestone, never allowing myself the grace to simply occupy the space I was in. Buster was the mirror I didn't know I needed.

In the stillness of my life, the noise of my past—the flight schedules, the TSA checkpoints, the shifting dynamics of family—began to quiet. I looked back at my life in the streets of San Francisco, the ringer-washing machine, and the streetlights that dictated my curfew. I realized that those early years had taught me to be constantly alert, but they hadn't taught me how to be still.

I learned that distilling life's wisdom isn't about gathering more luggage, more accolades, or more years; it is about the radical act of stripping away everything that obscures the truth. We spend our youth adding layers—degrees, titles, possessions, worries—as if we are building a fortress to protect our identity. But true strength, I have come to see, is found in the shedding of those layers.

Wisdom is not an accumulation; it is a subtraction. By the

time I left those mountains, I understood that the past isn't a burden to be carried, but a foundation to be walked upon with purpose. The mistakes of the past are not anchors; they are the markers on the map that tell us where we have been and where we must never go again.

I thought of the many flight paths I had charted over my career, the thousands of feet above the earth where the world looks like a map rather than a series of struggles. From that height, you see the interconnectedness of everything. But in the cabin, looking at the moss on the trees, I realized that living on the ground is just as vast.

There is a rhythm to the woods that matches the rhythm of a well-lived life. It requires the patience to let the seasons change and the humility to accept that we are not the masters of our own timeline. We are merely guests in our own existence, and the sooner we accept that, the freer we become.

My $400 Guittard chocolate/ restaurant bill felt like a failure at the time, but now it feels like a bargain. It was the entry fee to a new way of seeing the world. It taught me that failure is often just a perspective shift. If you are willing to look at your mistakes as teachers rather than judge them as shortcomings, you can turn any disaster into a revelation.

I wonder sometimes if the girl I was in San Francisco would recognize the woman who now finds such joy in silence. She was so hungry for the world, so desperate to fly away from the projects and see the horizon, that she might have thought the stillness of a cabin was a kind of prison. But she would have been wrong.

The freedom I sought in the skies is the same freedom I find in a quiet moment now. It is the freedom from the need to be busy, the need to impress, and the need to prove that I am more than the sum of my experiences. I am simply Natalie, and that is enough.

As I look toward my future—the travel I still crave, the law I hope to study, and the life I hope to build—I carry the spirit of the mountain with me. I do not need the fanfare to validate my journey, and I certainly do not need the expensive lettuce to teach me the value of preparation.

I am ready for whatever the mountain brings next. I have my map, I have my memories, and most importantly, I have the silence of the porch to remind me that as long as I am content in my own presence, I am exactly where I need to be.

The Art of the Slow Down

There is a specific, suffocating kind of violence in the relentless pace of modern life. We are taught from childhood that speed is a virtue, that productivity is the primary metric of worth, and that if you are not moving, you are falling behind. For decades, I lived in that "fast lane"—the grit of San Francisco, the thin, pressurized air of the skies, and the constant, jarring transition between foreign time zones and demanding, high-stakes schedules.

For the last few years, however, I have been focused on something else entirely: catching my breath. I realized that my life had become a series of arrivals and departures, where the middle, the substance of living, was merely a blur of clouds and runway tarmac. I had spent so much energy running toward the future that I had completely neglected to inhabit the present moment.

"The Art of the Slow Down" is not a passive surrender to inactivity; it is a deliberate, militant rebellion against a culture that demands we always be "on." It is the act of reclaiming one's own time. In a world that is constantly screaming for your attention, there is a profound, radical power in choosing to listen to the silence instead.

Living in a space that finally allows me to breathe—where there are no neighbors stacked on top of me, just the quiet, rhythmic architecture of trees and the gentle, rolling expanse of the golf course—has allowed me to finally reset my internal metronome. It is amazing how much of your own heartbeat you miss when you are constantly sprinting to keep up with the world's expectations.

I am learning to walk slower, to speak with intention rather than urgency, and to drive in a way that respects the journey rather than just the destination. This, I realize, is the necessary training for the next horizon. It isn't just about physical speed; it is about the pace at which I process the world.

Having spent my younger years as a "sponge," soaking up the vibrant, chaotic cultures of Morocco, the plains of Kenya, and the bustling, modern streets of Frankfurt, I am now finding that my greatest adventures are not found in new stamps on a passport. Instead, I am finding beauty in the stillness of a morning cup of coffee or the way the light shifts across my living room floor.

I remember the exhaustion of the cockpit—the long, heavy hauls across the Atlantic, the feet aching and swollen after hours of walking down narrow aisles, the constant responsibility of lives in my hands. Those memories are precious, but they are also a reminder of how much I asked of my body and my spirit during those years.

I remember the chance encounter with a pilot who offered to rub those tired, aching feet in the cockpit, a simple, human act of kindness that sparked a bond lasting 33 years. That moment was a pivot point. It taught me that even in the most technical, cold, and professional environments, grace can be found if you are willing to pause long enough to recognize it.

That man is my partner in this slow, intentional life. We have traveled the world together, navigating storms and clear skies alike, yet our greatest journey has been this one: learning to sit still together. It is a different kind of travel, one that doesn't require a boarding pass or an altitude adjustment.

I am learning that slowing down is the only way to carry the weight of the years with grace. When you move too fast, you drop things—you drop the details, the nuances, the small kindnesses that define a life. By slowing down, I can finally hold onto the things that truly matter.

It is the only way to ensure that we don't just exist, passing through days like travelers through check-in counters, but truly, deeply live. Existence is automatic; living is a choice. You have to decide, every single morning, that you are going to pay attention to the world around you rather than just rushing through it.

People often ask me if I miss the excitement of the flight attendant life, the rush of the jet-setting lifestyle. And while I cherish those memories, I explain that I have traded the external excitement for an internal peace. That peace is not empty; it is full of everything I finally have the time to notice.

The world will continue to spin at its frantic, breakneck speed, regardless of how fast I move. I have realized that I don't have to keep pace with it. I can step off the carousel whenever I want, and I can choose to set my own rhythm, governed only by the sunrise and the natural ebb and flow of my own soul.

As I look toward the years ahead, I do not fear the slowing down of my life. I welcome it. There is a dignity in a slower walk, a wisdom in a measured word, and a profound joy in a heart that no longer needs to race to feel alive. I am finally catching up to myself.

The flight, in many ways, is over, but the landing—the soft, deliberate transition to solid ground—is where I am finally finding my footing. I am not running toward a destination anymore. I am simply here, fully present, and for the first time in my life, that is more than enough.

Intergenerational Echoes

As I, Alexandria Roberts, sit here, a high school senior standing on the precipice of my own life, I find myself deeply changed by the stories Mrs. Natalie has shared. Reflecting on her journey—the long flights, the dangerous landings, and the quiet realizations in the mountains—I am struck most profoundly by her "loyalty to a fault." In a world that often rewards the transactional, seeing her unwavering commitment to those she loves, and even to those she has only just met, is a transformative lesson. Mrs. Natalie taught me that loyalty is not just a virtue; it is a heavy, beautiful armor that protects your character in a world that might otherwise wear it down.

Her stories of the "lost brother" and that harrowing "Saudi landing" have fundamentally shifted my understanding of resilience. I used to think resilience meant being impenetrable—a stone wall that nothing could crack. But through Mrs. Natalie's words, I see that true resilience is much more akin to the willow tree: it is the ability to bend, to sway with the turbulent winds of life, and yet remain rooted in one's own truth. She showed me that you can be terrified, you can be surrounded by the harsh reality of rifles in a jetway, and you can still choose to remain anchored in your purpose.

That perspective is exactly what I need as I prepare for the path ahead. I am a senior at Westlake High School, dreaming of the day I walk into a courtroom as a criminal defense attorney. Mrs. Natalie's stories has given me a roadmap I didn't know I was searching for. She has shown me that the law is not just about statutes and proceedings; it is about the humanity of the people involved. It is about navigating the complexities of justice with the same grace she navigated the complexities of global travel.

I want to extend a heartfelt, enduring thank you to Mrs. Natalie for the connection to her cousin. The bridge she built between us is more than just a contact; it is a testament to the intergenerational bond we share. It reminds me that I do not have to walk this path toward a Juris Doctor and a life of advocacy entirely on my own. I have the wisdom of those who have paved the way, and I have the example of Mrs. Natalie's life to guide my steps.

She has given me a vision of what a life of travel and service can look like. Whether I am advocating for a client in a courtroom or exploring a new country that I once only read about in textbooks, I will carry the "Art of the Slow Down" with me. I will remember that my career is a marathon, not a sprint, and that my worth is found in the depth of my impact, not the speed of my ascent.

Thank you, Mrs. Natalie, for being an architect of more than just your own history; you are helping me draft the blueprints for mine. As I head toward graduation and the next stage of my life at Miami University, I do so with the knowledge that the world is vast, but it is also accessible to those who are brave enough to hold their ground. You have helped me realize that being a lawyer is not just a job title—it is an opportunity to be a voice, a witness, and a guardian of the truth.

I am ready to carry the torch of our shared history. I am ready to explore, to learn, and to grow into the advocate I know I am capable of becoming. Mrs. Natalie has given me the confidence to step forward, and for that, I will be forever grateful. This is not the end of a story, but the beginning of a conversation that I hope to continue as I enter my own version of the professional world.

Her life has been a bridge for me, a way to cross the chasm between the uncertainty of youth and the focused, intentional future I desire. I have learned that the "right" answer is rarely found in a guidebook, but in the experiences we gather when we have the courage to venture off the beaten path. I will hold her stories close as I begin my undergraduate journey, using them as both a compass and a reminder to always be kind, to always be prepared, and to always, always be authentically myself.

As I look toward my future in law and travel, I know the road will be difficult, but I am no longer afraid of the detours. I see now that every "lost" moment is just another layer of the foundation I am building. Thank you, Mrs. Natalie, for showing me that beauty can be found in the most unexpected places and that every step, no matter how small, is a step toward becoming the woman I am meant to be.

The legacy you are building—one of curiosity, strength, and intentionality—is a legacy I am honored to carry forward. I will make sure that the path I pave for the next generation is just as meaningful, just as honest, and just as vibrant as the one you have walked for me. We are all, as you said, "just travelers," but some of us are lucky enough to have guides who light the way.

You are that guide for me, Mrs. Natalie, and I am stepping into this new season of my life with my head held high, my heart open, and a roadmap that is uniquely, undeniably mine. Thank you for everything. I am looking forward to making you proud as I begin to draft my own history, one chapter, one case, and one journey at a time.

-Alexandria Roberts
Class of 2026

Letter to Future Generations

I was born on November 30, 1954, at San Francisco General Hospital in San Francisco, California, to Adell and Louis. I began life in the Sunnydale projects neighborhood, growing up in the housing projects in a close-knit, working-class community.

My early life was shaped by family, both immediate and extended. My mother worked hard and held our household together. I had one older sister and two younger brothers who were close in age. My childhood was filled with family gatherings, BBQs, holidays, cousins, aunts, and uncles. My mother loved to entertain, and those moments created some of my strongest early memories.

Eventually, my family moved from the projects into our first home, and each home after that was better than the last. That progression taught me early that life can improve with effort, persistence, and direction.

As a child, I was shy. I was raised with the belief that children were to be seen and not heard. I became observant, quiet, and thoughtful. I had a best friend and early boyfriend named Dennis, and I formed four lifelong friendships in elementary school that I still have today.

Around the age of 8–10, I began visiting my father at my aunt's home. My parents were not married, but I was able to connect with my father and his large blended family, which included many siblings and step-siblings. This expanded my understanding of family and belonging.

My childhood also included painful and defining moments. At around age 9 or 10, I experienced harm from my stepfather. I told my brother, he told my mother, and she removed him from the home. That moment taught me that speaking up matters and that there can be protection when you tell the truth.

Another defining moment came later, when I was exposed to drugs in my environment. I had a clear moment of awareness and made the decision to walk away from that world. That choice shaped the direction of my entire life.

I learned early that your environment may influence you, but it does not have to define you. You will always face paths pulling you in different directions, but your decisions determine who you become.

I began working at Blue Cross Blue Shield processing claims. I was fired after misrepresenting my age so I could leave early to vote, but even that became part of my learning experience. I later worked at the Hyatt Regency in San Francisco, helping open the property and staying there for about five to six years. From there, I became a flight attendant—what I consider the best job I ever had. It gave me independence, growth, travel, and new experiences. It was also during this time that I met my husband.

I have now been married for over 34 years.

Looking back, my life has taught me several truths I want to pass on:

1. You do not start life on equal ground, but your beginning does not define your ending. I began in the projects, but life changed through movement, effort, and opportunity.

2. Family can be complicated, but it can also be protective. When I spoke up, I was heard. That matters.

3. Your choices matter more than your surroundings. I saw things in my environment that could have shaped a very different life for me, but I chose a different path.

4. Quiet people are not weak people. I was shy and observant, but I learned to make strong decisions and build a strong life.

5. Friendships and relationships are some of the most important anchors you will ever have. I still have friends from childhood, and I have a long marriage built over decades.

6. Work is not just survival—it can be growth, identity, and opportunity. My career path changed my life and led me to my husband.

7. Most importantly, life is not a straight line. It bends, changes, challenges you, and gives you chances to redirect. You can rebuild, rise, and choose again at any point.

If I could leave one message for future generations, it would be this:

You may not choose where you start in life, but you always have a choice in where you go. Speak up when something is wrong. Choose your direction carefully. Protect your relationships. Trust your ability to change your path. And never believe your beginning is your limit.

Wishing you a beautiful life,
Natalie Woods

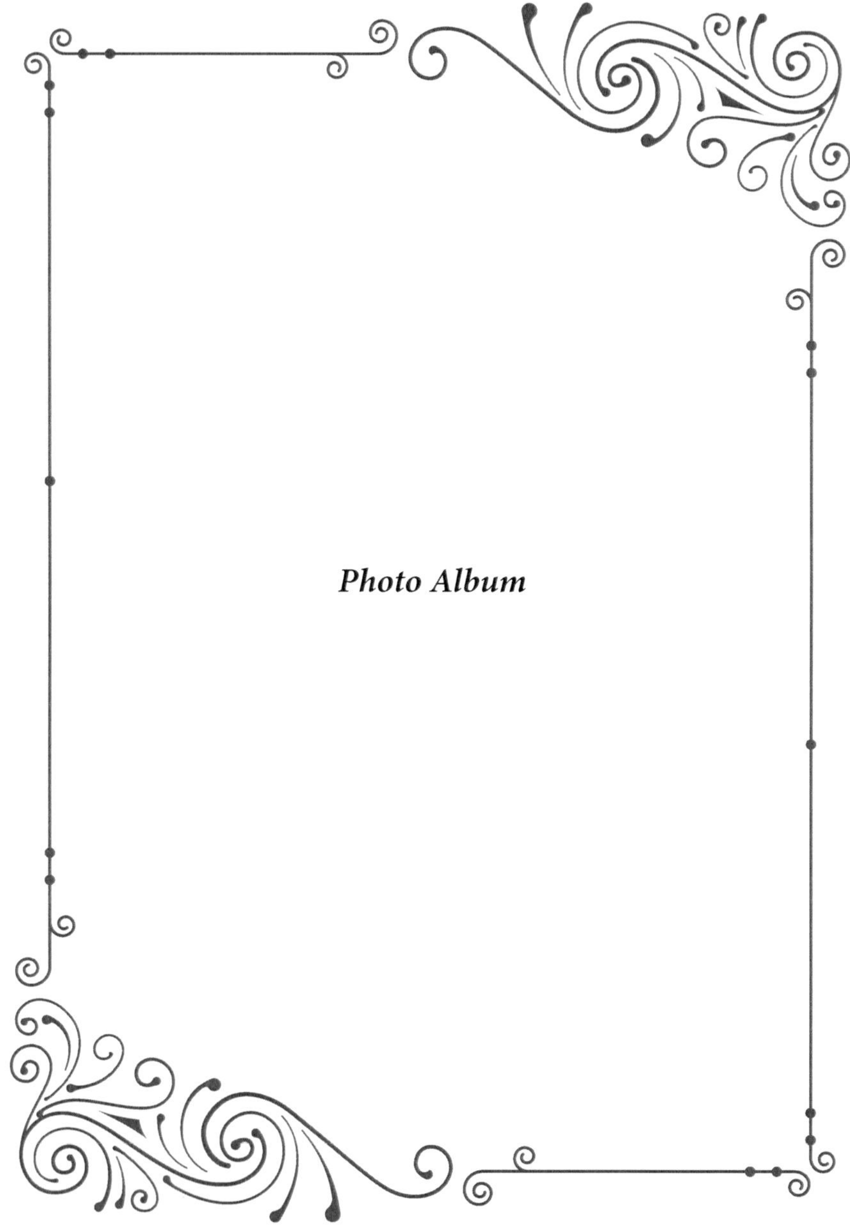

Photo Album

At one of my tea parties, around age 7 or 8.
I am the second child in from the left.

Me at our second home,
around age nine or ten.

Christmas at home.

Me at home at 14, in our third house
—a newly built home we lived in.

Me with my friend Denise, around age 14 or 15.
She was a beautiful soul who tragically passed away in a car accident.

Graduation from Aptos Junior High School.

Me with my sister, Fayetta Kelly Hartin.
She always went by Kelly—a name she chose for herself.

Me at one of the city's popular nightclubs,
The Vis. I was about 19 or 20 years old.

One of my first trips as a flight attendant, circa 1978.

My two self-adopted "sisters," Alta May Murdock and Bonny Jean Griffey, with me in the middle. We also flew together as flight attendants.

Helo deck Captains party on Equinox
Text
Happy in Santorini
Best friends in Lisbon
Hemingway bar
Lunch in Ephesus, Kusadas Turkey

Acknowledgements

I give thanks first to my mother, Adell, whose strength, love and determination held our family together and showed me what resilience looks like. Her ability to create a home filled with warmth, laughter, and family left a lasting imprint on my life.

To my siblings, who shared my early years and experiences, and to my extended family—my aunts, uncles, and cousins—thank you for the memories, the gatherings and the sense of who I am.

To my lifelong friends, the ones who have been with me since childhood, your presence through every stage of my life has been a true blessing. Few people are lucky enough to carry friendships across a lifetime, and I do not take that for granted.

To my husband, thank you for your love, partnership, and the life we have built together over the years. Meeting you changed my life in ways I will always cherish.

And finally, I acknowledge my younger self - the quiet, observant girl who found her way through difficult moments and chose a different path. This story is for her, and those who come after.

About the Author (Elder)

Natalie Woods is a woman of resilience, shaped by life's challenges and strengthened by her unwavering determination to rise above them. Her story is one of perseverance, growth, and the courage to keep moving forward even when the path is uncertain.

In Threads That Held Me Together, Natalie shares her journey with honesty and conviction, offering readers a powerful reminder that strength is often forged in the most difficult seasons. Her voice reflects both vulnerability and courage, inviting others to see themselves in her story and to believe in their own ability to overcome. She resides in Georgia and remains deeply rooted in faith, family, and purpose.

About the Author (Writer)

Alexandria Roberts is a graduating senior at Westlake High School and a proud rising freshman at Miami University, where she will begin her studies in the fall of 2026. Throughout her high school career, she has maintained a strong academic record, consistently earning a place on the A/B Honor Roll.

Her journey has been defined by a deep commitment to service, leadership, and personal growth. She is especially grateful for the opportunity to have met Mrs. Natalie Woods, an experience that has been meaningful in shaping her senior year. One of her most rewarding experiences has been participating in the "Senior to Senior" program, where she authored her first book. Through this initiative, she has woven together personal reflections—including themes such as the "Fog foundation"—into a narrative that captures her voice and lived experience.

Beyond her creative work, Alexandria has served as the soccer manager at Westlake for four years and has been a dedicated volunteer at the Nicholas Shelter Home since 2015. As she transitions to Miami University to pursue a double major in Political Science and Psychology, she looks forward to continuing to build on the resilience and storytelling skills she developed through this program. Her long-term goals include becoming a criminal defense attorney, while also pursuing her passion for the beauty industry as a future salon owner.

About Silver Bangles Productions

Silver Bangles Productions is an Atlanta-based storytelling and publishing studio dedicated to preserving memory, honoring legacy, and transforming lived experience into lasting narrative.

Founded by writer, filmmaker, and publisher Summer J. Robinson, Silver Bangles specializes in memoir, oral history, documentary storytelling, and intergenerational narrative work. Through books, film, educational programming, and archival projects, the company works to ensure that stories—particularly those rooted in Black communities, the African diaspora, the American South, and everyday lived experience—are documented with care, honesty, and dignity.

At Silver Bangles, storytelling is viewed as both art and preservation. The company believes that ordinary lives are worthy of documentation and that memory itself is a form of cultural inheritance. Whether publishing a memoir, producing a documentary, or facilitating a community storytelling program, Silver Bangles approaches each project with a commitment to narrative integrity, emotional truth, and historical preservation.

Silver Bangles Productions is also the home of Senior to Senior, an intergenerational storytelling initiative that pairs high school students with elders to co-create professionally published memoirs. The program was founded on the belief that storytelling can bridge generational divides, strengthen community, preserve oral history, and create healing through listening and reflection.

The studio's work exists at the intersection of publishing, education, documentary practice, and cultural preservation. Through collaborative storytelling, Silver Bangles seeks to create work that not only documents lives, but also affirms them.

Because stories matter, memory matters, and the people history often overlooks deserve to be remembered too.

Silver Bangles Productions
Atlanta, Georgia
www.silverbanglesproductions.com
info@silverbanglesproductions.com